This Journal Belongs To:

Tips for a Successful Gratitude Journal

- ## Focus on the Benefits:

Understand why your doing it before starting will make it easier for you to keep up the habit. The benefits of gratitude journaling include **lower stress levels**, a greater sense of **calm** and a whole new level of **clarity** in your life. You will learn more about yourself and be able to better focus your efforts on becoming the happiest version of yourself.

- ## Set Time Aside for Writing:

The easiest way to maintain a gratitude journal is by making it a habit. You should try attach it to an existing habit such as reading before bed or coffee in the morning.

- ## Start with Prompts

If your new to gratitude journaling it can be hard to think of what to write about. On the next page we have included a long list of gratitude prompts to help you think about what to be thankful for each day.

Gratitude Prompts:

- Hobbies you practice
- A moment that inspired you
- Places you visited
- Challenges you endured
- Water to drink
- The country you live in
- Activities you love
- Your heritage
- Your favorite vacations
- Your body
- Technology
- Books you love
- Food on the table
- Changes you've made
- Nature you explored
- Your elders
- A place to stay
- Your best friends
- Birthdays you've had
- Children in your life
- Events you attended

- Music you enjoy
- Your accomplishments
- Things you own
- Clothes you own
- Gifts you received
- Abilities you have
- Your colleagues
- Your best qualities
- Advice you received
- Simple things in your life
- A local spot you like
- People in your life
- Sunsets you've seen
- Risks you've taken
- Relationships you treasure
- Fears you overcame
- A person you love
- Your favorite memories
- Things you've learned
- Comfort you feel
- People you helped

"

It's Not Whether You Get Knocked Down, It's Whether You Get Up.
- Vince Lombardi

"

Date : _____

Today I am grateful for...

- _____
  _____
  _____

- _____
  _____
  _____

- _____
  _____
  _____

Describe your happiest childhood memory:

> *We can't help everyone, but everyone can help someone.*
> *- Ronald Reagan*

Date : _____

Today I am grateful for...

- _____

_____

_____

- _____

_____

_____

- _____

_____

_____

What do you love most about your country?:

Keep your face to the sunshine and you can never see the shadow.
— Helen Keller

Date : _____

Today I am grateful for...

- _____
_____
_____

- _____
_____
_____

- _____
_____
_____

Name 3 things that always put a smile on your face:

Date : _____

Today I am grateful for...

- _____
  _____
  _____

- _____
  _____
  _____

- _____
  _____
  _____

What is something you love(d) about your mother (or step-mother)?:

> *The aim of an argument or discussion*
> *should not be victory, but progress.*
> *— Joseph Joubert*

Date : _____

Today I am grateful for...

- _____
  _____
  _____

- _____
  _____
  _____

- _____
  _____
  _____

What do you really appreciate about your life?:

> *A person who never made a mistake never tried anything new.*
> *- Albert Einstein*

Date : _____

Today I am grateful for...

- _____
  _____
  _____

- _____
  _____
  _____

- _____
  _____
  _____

Who is a teacher or mentor that has made an
impact on your life and how did they help you?:

Date : _____

Today I am grateful for...

- _____
  _____
  _____

- _____
  _____
  _____

- _____
  _____
  _____

Where was your last vacation? Describe what you did there:

Week 1 Reflections

What I learned this week:

_____

_____

_____

_____

Best moments this week:

_____

_____

_____

_____

Anything to confess:

_____

_____

_____

What went well this week:

_____

_____

_____

_____

_____

What could have gone better:

_____

_____

_____

_____

_____

> *The only way to do great work is to love what you do.*
> *— Steve Jobs*

Date : _____

Today I am grateful for...

- _____
_____
_____

- _____
_____
_____

- _____
_____
_____

What are five personality traits that you are most thankful for?:

"

> *Certain things catch your eye, but pursue*
> *only those that capture the heart.*
> *- Ancient Indian Proverb*

"

Date : _____

Today I am grateful for...

- _____
  _____
  _____

- _____
  _____
  _____

- _____
  _____
  _____

What is your favorite holiday and why do you love it?:

> *Dream big and dare to fail.*
> *— Norman Vaughan*

Date : _____

Today I am grateful for...

- _____
  _____
  _____

- _____
  _____
  _____

- _____
  _____
  _____

Describe an experience that was painful, but made you a stronger person:

Date : _____

Today I am grateful for...

- _____
  _____
  _____
- _____
  _____
  _____
- _____
  _____
  _____

What is your favorite season and what do you like about it?:

Date : _____

Today I am grateful for...

- _____
  _____

- _____
  _____

- _____
  _____

What is a popular song that you enjoy (and why do you like it)?:

> *Don't be pushed by your problems. Be led by your dreams.*
> *— Ralph Waldo Emerson*

Date : _____

Today I am grateful for...

- _____

_____

_____

- _____

_____

_____

- _____

_____

_____

Describe your favorite smell:

> *Either you run the day, or the day runs you.*
> *— Jim Rohn*

Date : _____

Today I am grateful for...

- _____
_____
_____

- _____
_____
_____

- _____
_____
_____

What is your favorite sports team? Describe a cherished
memory you have when cheering for this team:

Week 2 Reflections

What I learned this week:

_____

_____

_____

_____

Best moments this week:

_____

_____

_____

_____

Anything to confess:

_____

_____

_____

What went well this week:

_____

_____

_____

_____

What could have gone better:

_____

_____

_____

_____

> *The best way out is always through.*
> — Robert Frost

Date : _____

Today I am grateful for...

- _____
  _____
  _____

- _____
  _____
  _____

- _____
  _____
  _____

What is your favorite memory of your father (or stepfather)?:

> *Success is going from failure to failure without losing your enthusiasm.*
> *— Winston Churchill*

Date : _____

Today I am grateful for...

- _____
  _____
  _____

- _____
  _____
  _____

- _____
  _____
  _____

How can you pamper yourself in the next 24 hours?:

> *Everything you've ever wanted is on the other side of fear.*
> — George Addair

Date : _____

Today I am grateful for...

- _____
  _____

- _____
  _____

- _____
  _____

What are your biggest accomplishments?:

> *If the wind will not serve, take to the oars.*
> — *Latin Proverb*

Date : _____

Today I am grateful for...

- _____
  _____
  _____

- _____
  _____
  _____

- _____
  _____
  _____

When was the last time you had a great nap where
you awoke feeling fully refreshed?:

Date : _____

Today I am grateful for...

- _____
  _____

- _____
  _____

- _____
  _____

Describe a family tradition that you are most grateful for:

> *Don't worry about failures, worry about the*
> *chances you miss when you don't even try.*
> *— Jack Canfield*

Date : _____

Today I am grateful for...

- _____

_____

_____

- _____

_____

_____

- _____

_____

_____

List 5 things you are looking forward to in the next year.

> *Tough times never last, but tough people do.*
> *— Dr. Robert Schuller*

Date : _____

Today I am grateful for...

- _____
_____
_____

- _____
_____
_____

- _____
_____
_____

What do other people like about you?:

Week 3 Reflections

What I learned this week:

_____

_____

_____

_____

Best moments this week:

_____

_____

_____

_____

Anything to confess:

_____

_____

_____

What went well this week:

_____

_____

_____

_____

What could have gone better:

_____

_____

_____

_____

Date : _____

Today I am grateful for...

- _____
_____
_____

- _____
_____
_____

- _____
_____
_____

List 10 items that you take for granted, which might
not be available to people in other parts of the world:

> *It's time to start living the life you've imagined*
> *— Henry James*

Date : _____

Today I am grateful for...

- _____
  _____
  _____

- _____
  _____
  _____

- _____
  _____
  _____

Three things about my health that have been going well for me are...

> *Always be a first-rate version of yourself,*
> *instead of a second-rate version of somebody else.*
> *— Judy Garland*

Date : _____

Today I am grateful for...

- _____
_____
_____

- _____
_____
_____

- _____
_____
_____

What is your favorite way to enjoy nature?:

Date : _____

Today I am grateful for...

- _____
  _____
  _____

- _____
  _____
  _____

- _____
  _____
  _____

What body part or organ are you most grateful for today?
(e.g., your eyes because you got to see a new movie):

Date : _____

Today I am grateful for...

- _____
  _____

- _____
  _____

- _____
  _____

I appreciate the following things about my job/work:

> *Remember that not getting what you want*
> *is sometimes a wonderful stroke of luck.*
> *- Dalai Lama*

Date : _____

Today I am grateful for...

- _____
  _____
  _____

- _____
  _____
  _____

- _____
  _____
  _____

Describe your favorite taste:

Date : _____

Today I am grateful for...

- _____
_____
_____

- _____
_____
_____

- _____
_____
_____

What is the biggest accomplishment in your professional life?:

Week 4 Reflections

What I learned this week:

_____

_____

_____

_____

Best moments this week:

_____

_____

_____

_____

Anything to confess:

_____

_____

_____

What went well this week:

_____

_____

_____

_____

What could have gone better:

_____

_____

_____

_____

Date : _____

Today I am grateful for...

- _____
- _____

- _____
- _____

- _____
- _____

Write about something you saw recently that warmed your heart:

Date : _____

Today I am grateful for...

- _____
- _____
- _____

What is your favorite part of your daily routine?:

> *Change your thoughts and you change your world.*
> — *Norman Vincent Peale*

Date : _____

Today I am grateful for...

- _____

_____

_____

- _____

_____

_____

- _____

_____

_____

Think about a time that you went out of your way to help someone:

> *An obstacle is often a stepping stone.*
> *— William Prescott*

Date : _____

Today I am grateful for...

- _____
  _____
  _____

- _____
  _____
  _____

- _____
  _____
  _____

A friend I cherish is _____, because he or she. . .

> *A year from now you may wish you had started today.*
> — *Karen Lamb*

Date : _____

Today I am grateful for...

- _____
  _____

- _____
  _____

- _____
  _____

What is your favorite quote or a bit of wisdom
that you like to frequently share with others?

Date : _____

Today I am grateful for...

- _____
- _____
- _____

What meals do you most enjoy making or eating?:

> *Life is what happens to you while you're busy making other plans.*
> — *John Lennon*

Date : _____

Today I am grateful for...

- _____

_____

- _____

_____

- _____

_____

The thing I love most about my town or city is. . .

Week 5 Reflections

What I learned this week:

_____

_____

_____

_____

Best moments this week:

_____

_____

_____

_____

Anything to confess:

_____

_____

_____

What went well this week:

_____

_____

_____

_____

What could have gone better:

_____

_____

_____

_____

> *Do what you love and the money will follow.*
> *— Marsha Sinetar*

Date : _____

Today I am grateful for...

- _____
  _____
  _____

- _____
  _____
  _____

- _____
  _____
  _____

One way I'm better today than I was one year ago is. . .

> *What lies behind us and what lies before us are*
> *tiny matters compared to what lies within us.*
> *— Henry S. Haskins*

Date : _____

Today I am grateful for...

- _____
_____
_____

- _____
_____
_____

- _____
_____
_____

List 3 people and/or things you feel that you take for granted. How can you express more appreciation for these things or people?:

Date : _____

Today I am grateful for...

- _____
_____
_____

- _____
_____
_____

- _____
_____
_____

One person I don't talk to very often, but I know I can count on is. . .

If you can't outplay them, outwork them.
— Ben Hogan

Date : _____

Today I am grateful for...

- _____

_____

_____

- _____

_____

_____

- _____

_____

_____

What aspects of your job do you enjoy the most?:

> *You must not only aim right, but draw the bow with all your might.*
> — *Henry David Thoreau*

Date : _____

Today I am grateful for...

- _____
  _____

- _____
  _____

- _____
  _____
  _____

One song I love is _____ because. . .

> *Nothing will work unless you do.*
> *—Maya Angelou*

Date: _____

Today I am grateful for...

- _____
  _____

- _____
  _____

- _____
  _____

One thing that always makes me feel better when I'm down is. . .

Date : _____

Today I am grateful for...

- _____
- _____
- _____

One of my most worthwhile purchases has been my. . .

Week 6 Reflections

What I learned this week:

_____

_____

_____

_____

Best moments this week:

_____

_____

_____

_____

Anything to confess:

_____

_____

_____

What went well this week:

_____

_____

_____

_____

What could have gone better:

_____

_____

_____

_____

> *Few things can help an individual more than to place responsibility on him, and to let him know that you trust him.*
> *— Booker T. Washington*

Date : _____

Today I am grateful for...

- _____
  _____
  _____

- _____
  _____
  _____

- _____
  _____
  _____

List 3 things you have now that you didn't have 5 years ago:

> *You can't use up creativity. The more you use, the more you have.*
> *- Maya Angelou*

Date : _____

Today I am grateful for...

- _____
_____
_____

- _____
_____
_____

- _____
_____
_____

Name 3 things you are doing well currently:

> *I am not a product of my circumstances.*
> *I am a product of my decisions.*
> *- Stephen Covey*

Date : _____

Today I am grateful for...

- _____
  _____
  _____

- _____
  _____
  _____

- _____
  _____
  _____

One freedom I often take for granted is. . .

> *Every strike brings me closer to the next home run.*
> — Babe Ruth

Date : _____

Today I am grateful for...

- _____
  _____
  _____

- _____
  _____
  _____

- _____
  _____
  _____

What physical characteristics are you most grateful for?:

> *Never let your memories be greater than your dreams.*
> — Doug Ivester

Date : _____

Today I am grateful for...

- _____
  _____

  _____

- _____
  _____

  _____

- _____
  _____

  _____

What family members are you most grateful for?
Write about what makes them special:

> *The most common way people give up their power*
> *is by thinking they don't have any.*
> *- Alice Walker*

Date : _____

Today I am grateful for...

- _____
  _____
  _____

- _____
  _____
  _____

- _____
  _____
  _____

When was the last time you had a genuine belly laugh
and why was it so funny?:

> *It wasn't raining when Noah built the ark.*
> *— Howard Ruff*

Date : _____

Today I am grateful for...

- _____
  _____
  _____

- _____
  _____
  _____

- _____
  _____
  _____

What activity do you enjoy when with others?:

Week 7 Reflections

What I learned this week:

_____

_____

_____

_____

Best moments this week:

_____

_____

_____

_____

Anything to confess:

_____

_____

_____

What went well this week:

_____

_____

_____

_____

What could have gone better:

_____

_____

_____

_____

Date : _____

Today I am grateful for...

- _____
  _____
  _____

- _____
  _____
  _____

- _____
  _____
  _____

Are you a morning person or a night owl? What do you love most about this part of the day?:

> *What we fear doing most is usually what we most need to do.*
> *— Tim Ferriss*

Date : _____

Today I am grateful for...

- _____
  _____
  _____

- _____
  _____
  _____

- _____
  _____
  _____

Write the top 3 things in your life that cause you stress.
For each stress factor, write what you can do to change it.

> *You make a living by what you get; you make a life by what you give.*
> *— Winston Churchill*

Date : _____

Today I am grateful for...

- _____
  _____
  _____

- _____
  _____
  _____

- _____
  _____
  _____

What is your favorite food you love to indulge in?:

> *Nurture your mind with great thoughts.*
> *To believe in the heroic makes heroes.*
> *- Benjamin Disraeli*

Date : _____

Today I am grateful for...

- _____
  _____
  _____

- _____
  _____
  _____

- _____
  _____
  _____

My favorite way to exercise is _____ because when I do it, I feel. . .

> *Just keep going. Everybody gets better if they keep at it.*
> *— Ted Williams*

Date : _____

Today I am grateful for...

- _____
_____
_____

- _____
_____
_____

- _____
_____
_____

One thing I love about my daily schedule is that. . .

> *What's money? A man is a success if he gets up in the morning and goes to bed at night and in between does what he wants to do.*
> *- Bob Dylan*

Date : _____

Today I am grateful for...

- _____
  _____

- _____
  _____

- _____
  _____
  _____

Describe a favorite pet and what you love(d) about it.

Just know, when you truly want success, you'll never give up on it.
No matter how bad the situation may get.
— Unknown

Date : _____

Today I am grateful for...

- _____
  _____
  _____

- _____
  _____
  _____

- _____
  _____
  _____

Are you happy with how your day turned out?:

Week 8 Reflections

What I learned this week:

_____

_____

_____

_____

Best moments this week:

_____

_____

_____

_____

Anything to confess:

_____

_____

_____

What went well this week:

_____

_____

_____

_____

What could have gone better:

_____

_____

_____

_____

> *Life is what we make it, always has been, always will be.*
> *— Grandma Moses*

Date : _____

Today I am grateful for...

- _____
  _____
  _____

- _____
  _____
  _____

- _____
  _____
  _____

What are you most looking forward to this week?:

"

> *Perfection is not attainable,*
> *but if we chase perfection we can catch excellence.*
> *- Vince Lombardi*

"

Date : _____

Today I am grateful for...

- _____
- _____
- _____

Write about a recent obstacle you faced and how you overcame it:

> *Alone, we can do so little; together we can do so much.*
> *- Helen Keller*

Date : _____

Today I am grateful for...

- _____
  _____
  _____

- _____
  _____
  _____

- _____
  _____
  _____

What is one of your favorite songs from your childhood?:

Date : _____

Today I am grateful for...

- _____
_____
_____

- _____
_____
_____

- _____
_____
_____

What is today's weather and what is one positive thing you can say about it?:

> *Even if you're on the right track, you'll get run over*
> *if you just sit there.*
> *— Will Rogers*

Date : _____

Today I am grateful for...

- _____
  _____
  _____

- _____
  _____
  _____

- _____
  _____
  _____

I know I'm not alone in this life because. . .

> *Whatever the mind of man can conceive and believe, it can achieve.*
> *- Napoleon Hill*

Date : _____

Today I am grateful for...

- _____
  _____
  _____

- _____
  _____
  _____

- _____
  _____
  _____

What makes you beautiful?:

> *Strive not to be a success, but rather to be of value.*
> *- Albert Einstein*

Date : _____

Today I am grateful for...

- _____
  _____
  _____

- _____
  _____
  _____

- _____
  _____
  _____

What are a few aspects of modern technology that you love?:

Week 9 Reflections

What I learned this week:

_____

_____

_____

_____

_____

Best moments this week:

_____

_____

_____

_____

Anything to confess:

_____

_____

_____

What went well this week:

_____

_____

_____

_____

What could have gone better:

_____

_____

_____

_____

> *To handle yourself, use your head; to handle others, use your heart.*
> *- Eleanor Roosevelt*

Date : _____

Today I am grateful for...

- _____
  _____
  _____

- _____
  _____
  _____

- _____
  _____
  _____

What is your favorite habit and why it is an important part of your daily routine?:

> *The best way to predict the future is to invent it.*
> — *Alan Kay*

Date : _____

Today I am grateful for...

- _____
  _____
  _____

- _____
  _____
  _____

- _____
  _____
  _____

What 3 things you love about the town, area or neighborhood you live in?:

> *Change your thoughts and you change your world.*
> *- Norman Vincent Peale*

Date : _____

Today I am grateful for...

- _____
  _____
  _____

- _____
  _____
  _____

- _____
  _____
  _____

My favorite adventure/vacation was _____ because. . .

> *The journey of a thousand miles begins with one step.*
> *— Lao Tzu*

Date : _____

Today I am grateful for...

- _____
- _____
- _____

Describe a funny YouTube video that you recently watched:

> *I've learned that people will forget what you said, people will forget what you did, but people will never forget how you made them feel.*
> *- Maya Angelou*

Date : _____

Today I am grateful for...

- _____
  _____
  _____

- _____
  _____
  _____

- _____
  _____
  _____

One piece of advice or a quote that has stayed with me is. . .

> *Don't wait. The time will never be just right.*
> *— Napoleon Hill*

Date : _____

Today I am grateful for...

- _____
_____
_____

- _____
_____
_____

- _____
_____
_____

What artist, musician or author are you most grateful for?:

Date : _____

Today I am grateful for...

- _____
- _____
- _____

How have you recently cared for your mental wellbeing?:

Week 10 Reflections

What I learned this week:

_____

_____

_____

_____

Best moments this week:

_____

_____

_____

_____

Anything to confess:

_____

_____

_____

What went well this week:

_____

_____

_____

_____

What could have gone better:

_____

_____

_____

_____

> *Someday is not a day of the week.*
> *— Denise Brennan-Nelson*

Date : _____

Today I am grateful for...

- _____
  _____
  _____

- _____
  _____
  _____

- _____
  _____
  _____

What is a favorite country that you've visited?:

> *Life is 10 percent what happens to me*
> *and 90 percent of how I react to it.*
> *- Charles Swindoll*

Date : _____

Today I am grateful for...

- _____
  _____

- _____
  _____

- _____
  _____

What do you love most about the current season?"

Date : _____

Today I am grateful for...

- _____
_____
_____

- _____
_____
_____

- _____
_____
_____

Describe the last time you procrastinated on a task
that wasn't as difficult as you thought it would be:

> *A truly rich man is one whose children run*
> *into his arms when his hands are empty.*
> *- Unknown*

Date : _____

Today I am grateful for...

- _____
_____
_____

- _____
_____
_____

- _____
_____
_____

What is something nice another person did for you today or this week?:

Date : _____

Today I am grateful for...

- _____
  _____
  _____

- _____
  _____
  _____

- _____
  _____
  _____

What is one lesson you learn from rude people?:

> *Make each day your masterpiece.*
> *— John Wooden*

Date : _____

Today I am grateful for...

- _____
  _____
  _____

- _____
  _____
  _____

- _____
  _____
  _____

What is the biggest lesson you learned in childhood?:

> *The creation of a thousand forests is in one acorn.*
> *– Ralph Waldo Emerson*

Date : _____

Today I am grateful for...

- _____
_____
_____

- _____
_____
_____

- _____
_____
_____

One talent I have been blessed with is. . .

Week 11 Reflections

What I learned this week:

_____

_____

_____

_____

Best moments this week:

_____

_____

_____

_____

Anything to confess:

_____

_____

_____

What went well this week:

_____

_____

_____

_____

What could have gone better:

_____

_____

_____

_____

> *If you want to lift yourself up, lift up someone else.*
> *- Booker T. Washington*

Date : _____

Today I am grateful for...

- _____
  _____
  _____

- _____
  _____
  _____

- _____
  _____
  _____

My favorite thing about coming home at the end of the day is. . .

"The only person you are destined to
become is the person you decide to be.
- Ralph Waldo Emerson

Date : _____

Today I am grateful for...

- _____
_____
_____
- _____
_____
_____
- _____
_____
_____

List 3 things you love about your home:

Date : _____

Today I am grateful for...

- _____
  _____
  _____

- _____
  _____
  _____

- _____
  _____
  _____

What is a personal viewpoint that positively defines you as a person?:

Limitations live only in our minds.
But if we use our imaginations, our possibilities become limitless.
— Jamie Paolinetti

Date : _____

Today I am grateful for...

- _____
_____
_____

- _____
_____
_____

- _____
_____
_____

Describe your favorite location in your house and why you like it:

> "
> *We can easily forgive a child who is afraid of the dark;*
> *the real tragedy of life is when men are afraid of the light.*
> *—Plato*
> "

Date : _____

Today I am grateful for...

- _____
- _____
- _____

Did you have a nice surprise today? Write about it:

> *The more I want to get something done,*
> *the less I call it work.*
> *— Richard Bach*

Date : _____

Today I am grateful for...

- _____
  _____
  _____

- _____
  _____
  _____

- _____
  _____
  _____

One piece of technology I can't live without is. . .

> *I alone cannot change the world, but I can cast a*
> *stone across the water to create many ripples.*
> *—Mother Teresa*

Date : _____

Today I am grateful for...

- _____
  _____
  _____

- _____
  _____
  _____

- _____
  _____
  _____

Describe your favorite sound:

Week 12 Reflections

What I learned this week:

_____

_____

_____

_____

Best moments this week:

_____

_____

_____

_____

Anything to confess:

_____

_____

_____

What went well this week:

_____

_____

_____

_____

What could have gone better:

_____

_____

_____

_____

> *Never give up on something that you can't go*
> *a day without thinking about.*
> *— Unknown*

Date : _____

Today I am grateful for...

- _____
  _____
  _____

- _____
  _____
  _____

- _____
  _____
  _____

What is your favorite charity and why do you support it?:

> *The real opportunity for success lies within*
> *the person and not in the job.*
> *- Zig Ziglar*

Date : _____

Today I am grateful for...

- _____
  _____
  _____

- _____
  _____
  _____

- _____
  _____
  _____

An artist or author whose body of work continually inspires me is. . .

> *I would rather die of passion than of boredom.*
> *- Vincent van Gogh*

Date : _____

Today I am grateful for...

- _____
  _____
  _____

- _____
  _____
  _____

- _____
  _____
  _____

One way I have bettered myself in the past month is. . .

> *It is never too late to be what you might have been.*
> — George Eliot

Date : _____

Today I am grateful for...

- _____
  _____
  _____

- _____
  _____
  _____

- _____
  _____
  _____

What is a great book you've recently read?:

I will go anywhere as long as it is forward.
– David Livingston

Date :_____

Today I am grateful for...

- _____
  _____
  _____

- _____
  _____
  _____

- _____
  _____
  _____

What is a favorite drink that you like to enjoy each day?:

Don't wish it were easier, wish you were better.
— Jim Rohn

Date : _____

Today I am grateful for...

- _____
  _____
  _____

- _____
  _____
  _____

- _____
  _____
  _____

List 3 things you could do today to be a kinder person:

> *If you're offered a seat on a rocket ship,*
> *don't ask what seat! Just get on.*
> *— Sheryl Sandberg*

Date : _____

Today I am grateful for...

- _____
  _____
  _____

- _____
  _____
  _____

- _____
  _____
  _____

How is your life more positive today than it was a year ago?:

Week 13 Reflections

What I learned this week:

_____

_____

_____

_____

Best moments this week:

_____

_____

_____

_____

Anything to confess:

_____

_____

_____

What went well this week:

_____

_____

_____

_____

What could have gone better:

_____

_____

_____

_____

3 Month Reflection

What was my greatest accomplishment:

_____

_____

_____

_____

What am I spending too little/too much time on? :

_____

_____

_____

_____

What didn't go to plan and how can I improve it? :

_____

_____

_____

_____

What do I want to achieve in the next 3 months? :

_____

_____

_____

_____

Congratulations on completing
your 90 day gratitude journal.

Don't let the journey end here..

You can find the next edition On
our Amazon Author Page.

Follow us on Instagram or Facebook
to see our latest releases.

www.instagram.com/PrettyNiftyPlanners
www.facebook.com/PrettyNiftyPlanners

Pretty Nifty
Planners

Made in the USA
Monee, IL
20 March 2020